Time Out
for Teachers

Also by Marjory Goldfinch Ward

Time Out for Teachers

Marjory Goldfinch Ward

Baker Books

A Division of Baker Book House Co
Grand Rapids, Michigan 49516

© 1998 by Marjory Goldfinch Ward

Published by Baker Books
a division of Baker Book House Company
P.O. Box 6287, Grand Rapids, MI 49516-6287

Printed in the United States of America

Library of Congress Cataloging-in-Publication Data

Ward, Marjory G. (Marjory Goldfinch)
    Time out for teachers / Marjory Goldfinch Ward.
        p.   cm.
    ISBN 0-8010-1168-X (hardcover)
        1. Teachers—Prayer-books and devotions—English. 2. Educa-
tion (Christian theology)—Meditations. 3. Devotional calendars.
I. Title.
BV4596.T43W365   1998
242'.88—dc21   98-14902

Contents

Introduction

Two-year-old Kaci vented her frustrations by biting another child. Her teacher corrected her behavior by giving her a time out in a little chair away from the other children. Kaci had to sit still and be quiet until a timer went off. Then she could return to the group, tell the other child she was sorry, get a big hug from the teacher, and run off to play again. At home, Kaci's parents reinforce the strategy, using it when Kaci disobeys or acts in an unacceptable way.

Teachers can "act ugly" too, at times. We get angry and frustrated, ready to lash out at the nearest person. We, like Kaci, need a time out—to recognize who is in charge, to think over our actions, to prepare to say, "I'm sorry," and to get ready for a big hug from our Teacher, who loves us most.

These devotions provide for time out—brief periods of reflection on the things that matter most in the challenging task that is ours.

Be still [get quiet] and know [remember] that
  I am God.

Psalm 46:10

7

Tell Me How to Behave

He who despises the word brings destruction
   on himself,
   but he who respects the commandment
   will be rewarded.

Proverbs 13:13 RSV

As school began one fall, students in a particular class suggested basic rules to follow and discussed the consequences of breaking the rules. The results were posted on the classroom wall:

Discipline Plan

1. Respect all adults and peers.
2. Be prepared for class at all times.
3. Talk only at appropriate times.
4. Follow directions and stay on task.

5. Sit correctly at your desk.
6. Keep hands, feet, and objects to yourself.
7. Do not tease, tattle, or use bad language.

Consequences

1. Name on the board: warning
2. One check by name: lose a half recess
3. Two checks by name: lose all recess
4. Three checks by name: parent contacted
5. Four checks by name: principal's office

Rewards

1. Good behavior all day: a smiley face on chart
2. Good behavior all week: a treat
3. Good behavior for six weeks: a BIG surprise!

Teachers know the importance of rules. Without rules that are understood and accepted, classrooms become chaotic, teachers cannot teach effectively, and students cannot learn.

I sometimes wish God would send me a poster outlining his rules for my behavior. It would be better still if he would discuss these rules with me and let me know exactly what the consequences will be if I violate his rules.

I am uncomfortably aware that he has already done that. Every time I read the Bible I see clear guidelines for my behavior. Here are some of the rules I have found:

Be kind to each other.
Be content with what you have.
Forgive each other.
Pray for each other.
Do what you would like others to do for you.
Stand up against evil.
Be careful what you say.
Be patient.
Be thankful.
Love God with all your heart.
Love your neighbor as yourself.

And here are some of the consequences:

First offense: The still, small voice of conscience will warn you, "You're headed for trouble."
Second offense: This behavior can be habit forming. Lose some of your peace and freedom.
Third offense: Lose peace until you seek forgiveness.
Fourth offense: God will send his Holy Spirit to confront you.
Fifth offense: Face God's judgment for rebellion.

And the rewards:

Consistent obedience: a "smiley face" representing peace, for "great peace have they who love your law" (Ps. 119:165)
Continuing obedience: surprising blessings

Anna, at the age of four, announced that she did not plan to go to school. When her parents suggested that she would have to go when she turned five, she said, "Then I'll just sit there and do nuffin."

Her older brother warned, "You'll be sent to the principal's office."

She tossed her curls. "Then I'll just talk uggy."

Anna is now happily involved in kindergarten, an eager, model student, with no "uggy talking" or "doing nuffin." She is learning quickly that when she follows the rules, school is more enjoyable.

Rules make life better for us all, not just in the classroom but in all of life. When we don't follow God's rules, our lives become chaotic and we cannot effectively learn and experience all the wonderful things God wants to teach us and give to us. His rules, like the rules of a classroom, are meant to help us not harm us.

But be doers of the word, and not hearers only, deceiving yourselves. For if any one is a hearer of the word and not a doer, he is like a man who observes his natural face in a mirror; for he observes himself and goes away and at once forgets what he was like. But he who looks into the perfect law, the law of liberty, and perseveres, being no hearer that forgets but a doer that acts, he shall be blessed in the doing.

James 1:22–25 RSV

Father-Teacher,

Forgive our foolish rebellion
against your rules
when they interfere with our ways
of thinking and behaving.
We were born selfish;
we have to learn how to be
gentle and kind,
patient and forgiving,
when everything inside screams
for its own way
no matter how cruelly
that way can hurt other people.
Set a seal on my lips.
Clean out the meanness inside me,
the bitterness,
the wrath,
the malice
that beg to lash out and hurt.
Give to me a gentle spirit,
a caring, quiet spirit
that spreads peace across turmoil
and centers its quietness in my own heart.

2
feed the
Sheep

And the vessel he was making of clay was spoiled in the potter's hand, and he reworked it into another vessel, as it seemed good to the potter to do.

Jeremiah 18:4 RSV

ebbie and Rick recently returned from several years as missionaries in Tanzania. Debbie is now a speech therapist in a public school. She said, "I love my work, but I am swamped with the papers I have to fill out." She added, "I haven't found a ministry yet. In the church, that is."

Astonished, I blurted out, "You have a ministry with those students!"

Debbie smiled. "I thought about that when I checked their records. I see child abuse victims, children from dysfunctional families—many with a variety of handicaps." She added thoughtfully, "I guess my work *is* 'ministry,' isn't it?"

Debbie works one-on-one with children who need, more than anything, the love of Christ Jesus that flows through her. God has prepared her life as a vessel for his own use.

The vessel God forms of each life can be used to give food and drink to his sheep.

I can ornament, polish, and protect the vessel of my life to such an extent that it becomes too valuable to use and fail to notice that it holds nothing to offer to sheep.

Or I may choose to keep it safe, away from the sheep. But what good are food and water, or the vessels that hold them, if the sheep can't get to them?

Three times Jesus asked, "Peter, do you love me?" Peter answered, "Yes, Lord, you know I love you." Three times Jesus commanded, "Feed my sheep" (John 21).

My students are my sheep. As I give to them, I am also showing my love for Christ.

Father,

*I have notions of my own
about the type of vessel
I want to be
and where I want to be placed.*

I tend to think that some sheep
are more valuable than others,
and some pastures are certainly
more comfortable.
Let me not forget that you are the potter.
My life is the work of your hands
or it is nothing.
I am obedient
or I am nothing.
When the sheep are feeding from the vessel
and I fear that there will be nothing left,
remind me that you fill the vessel
with food,
and you will replenish the supply.

3
Take Me to the Circus!

This morning gives promise to the rise of a glorious day.

William Shakespeare

This is the day which the LORD has made;
let us rejoice and be glad in it!
Psalm 118:24 RSV

The joy of the LORD is your strength!
Nehemiah 8:10 RSV

Paul thanked God and took courage.
Acts 28:15

Clark Morphew, in his article "A First Christmas without Mom" written for *The State* newspaper, said, "We didn't have much, but we always went to the circus!"

Steve and Kathy Murray, with their daughters, Megi and Carroll, came to visit our college class one day. Seventeen years ago, when Steve was twenty-one years old, he broke his neck in a diving accident. Since that time he has been a paraplegic. He and Kathy married not long after the accident. They have a close, happy, hardworking family, and they do what they have to do to make their lives work. Their attitude is "We take the good and make the most of it."

Michelle Harter has cerebral palsy. As far as Michelle is concerned, her problem with her legs is the least important thing about her. She plunges headlong into life and has a great time. She says, "God showed me Genesis 1:27, and that was all I needed to know. He created me, so it doesn't matter what the world thinks as long as I am pleasing him." Her special verse, and she lives it out, is "I can do everything through him who gives me strength" (Phil. 4:13). Michelle knows how to "go to the circus" and take others with her because she chooses to live a life of joy. The circus is a place of laughter and fun. Those who "go to the circus" refuse to let life rob them of the joy that is available.

God wants us to find joy in all circumstances, even those we may find difficult or unpleasant. This is possible, for Habakkuk reminds us that no matter how tough life is, we can walk with "hinds' feet"—be surefooted in tricky places—for our strength is in the Lord our God (Hab. 3:19 RSV). No matter what our circumstances, God gives us his "eternal encouragement" (2 Thess. 2:16).

Like the hardpressed family that always found money for the circus, we too can look for joy in spite of our circumstances.

Faith keeps up its courage.

Hebrews 10:23

Be strong . . . and work. For I am with you. . . . my Spirit remains among you. Do not fear.

Haggai 2:4–5

Father,

> Sometimes I simply don't feel like
> buying a ticket to the circus.
> I'd rather sit in my corner
> and invite other people to my pity party.
> My life is complex.
> The load becomes too heavy to carry.
> I don't feel lighthearted,
> and I don't know how to feel lighthearted.
> Somehow I don't think that lightheartedness
> is an appropriate response
> to this dreadful world.
> I know I need to laugh
> and sing
> and dance.

But how can I, in my situation?
By casting my burden on you, Lord.
You will sustain me;
you will set me free to laugh again,
and sing again,
and dance in your presence.

Light
a Candle

You are the light of the world.

Matthew 5:14

Ever since he was in the third grade, Jeff, now father of his own three young children, has loved to read: "My third-grade teacher always brought us back into the classroom after recess, lit a big candle, and read to us from books like *Huckleberry Finn*. After each day's reading, one child got to blow out the candle. We always vied with each other for the privilege of blowing out that candle!"

He adds, "Now I read to my daughters every night before they go to sleep. We light a big candle, get up on the bed, and I read them stories."

One teacher. One candle. Stories.

I wonder how many of that teacher's former students now read stories to their children by the light of a big candle.

When our first grandchild, Andrew, was born, his aunt Nancy gave us Richard Scarry's *Cars and Trucks and Things That Go*. On every page the artist has hidden a tiny goldbug for the child to locate. We read that book to Andrew and then to each of our other grandchildren as they came along. When the first copy fell apart, we replaced it with a new one. Each family now has its own copy!

Recently Andrew, now ten, and his sister Libby, who is seven, came to spend the night with us. They went for the "goldbug book," but this time Andrew read it to Libby himself. We have many children's books to choose from, but that one has become the all-time favorite.

My mother loved books by Charles Dickens, especially *David Copperfield*. Every fall, when the air turned cool and the sky was overcast, she would say, "It's time for me to visit with my friends the McCawbers!" I was forty years old before I learned to appreciate her love for the McCawbers. My mother also loved the Bible. She studied it, taught it, and read it every day. As a child, I was astonished at her devotion to such a boring looking old book, but I noticed what a difference it made in her life.

Now I understand. I meet the friends she met there, and I draw strength from the words that gave her strength. She lit a candle for me that has never gone out.

A city on a hill cannot be hidden. In the same way, let your light shine before men, that they may see your good deeds and praise your Father in heaven.

Matthew 5:14–16

Father,

> Thank you for the candles
>   others have lit for me.
> Thank you for the bright, big candle
>   Mama lit for me
> when she taught me by her example
> to love the Bible and live by its teachings.
> Thank you for all the children who love to read
>   because a parent, or a teacher,
>   lit that candle.
>   Thank you most of all
>   for the light of your love
>   that has been turned on
>   in the lives of those
>   whose teachers loved them,
>   believed in them,
>   and let them know it.

5 Enter Where God Calls

For you know the grace of our Lord Jesus Christ, that though he was rich, yet for your sakes he became poor, so that you through his poverty might become rich.

2 Corinthians 8:9

When he was eighteen months old, Marcus began rocking back and forth, retreating into his solitary world, endlessly and obsessively twirling a cookie or a plate on the floor, in frightening ways establishing the fact that he was autistic. Experts everywhere said to the anguished parents, "Bring him back in three or four years. He's too young to work with now."

The parents and their older children determined to enter the autistic world with Marcus. "If he can't come out to us, we'll go in to him," they maintained. The members of the family took turns entering his world.

They went into the bathroom with Marcus (his favorite room because it was the most set apart). They rocked when he rocked, twirled as he twirled, and tried to feel as he felt.

After 9,600 hours Marcus ventured out and began to relate normally to his family and other people. After an interval of normality he reverted briefly into his autistic state, and again his family shared his bizarre behaviors.

When Marcus again emerged from his isolation, he remained stable and developed into a normal, gregarious child.

When I think of the coming into the world of God's Son, I think of Marcus. God, seeing us in our "autism"—our confusion, our mindless behaviors, our self-imposed isolation from God's love and the warmth of his family—loved us too much to leave us alone. Determined to draw us into his world, he entered into our limited, unaware, wretched state and joined in the behaviors normal to that state.

He talked of the eternal and the indescribable in the limited language we could grasp. He shared the limitations of a physical body to the point of death and burial so that we could follow him into the abundant life that was his own normality.

For God so loved that he could not leave us alone, but gave himself over to human existence, that whoever of us perceives his love and responds should not perish in our separated condition, but will enter into the fullness of his own eternal dimension.

In what other way could the autistic child have learned that his mother, father, and siblings loved him if they had not cared enough to take on the limitations of his prison?

In what other way could we have learned that God loves us if he had not cared enough to take on the limitations of our self-imposed prison in order to free us from sin? He "knows that we are dust" and became dust with us, that we might experience life that is eternal, released from our isolation and free to live the life he calls us to. God wants us to be like Jesus in this respect, humbly entering where he calls us.

> Your attitude should be the same as that of
> Christ Jesus:
> Who, being in very nature God,
> did not consider equality with God
> something to be grasped,
> but made himself nothing,
> taking the very nature of a servant,
> being made in human likeness.
> And being found in appearance as a man,
> he humbled himself

and became obedient unto death—even
death on a cross!

Philippians 2:5–8

Father-Rescuer,

You saw us when we drew away from you.
You grieved over our lonely isolation.
You recognized the twisting
inside our deepest selves
that caused our withdrawal
and our mindless behaviors.
You could get our attention
only by coming into our affliction.
You sent your Son, your beloved,
to shut himself off from glory and majesty
and to enter into the limitations
of fallen flesh.
Thank you that Jesus won the victory—
he broke the bars of our imprisonment
and cast off the chains of our enslavement.
When my students draw away from me
and trouble fills their eyes with sadness,
help me to enter into their darkness
that I may share the light of life.

6 Take Hold of God's Hand

Now faith is being sure of what we hope for and certain of what we do not see.

Hebrews 11:1

Faith gropes in the darkness for the hand you know is there, and grasps it.

Anonymous

It's not that I believe that God is dead, it's just that I think he's an underachiever.

Woody Allen

When a student fails to live up to what we expect of him, based on his ability level, we call the student an underachiever. Usually the student is following his own agenda, accomplishing his own goals. He may be succeeding at what he really wants to do, even if he is failing to measure up to our goals for him.

We know that God is all-powerful. We also know that there are things he could do that he does not do. But God said plainly, "My ways are not your ways." He may have an agenda very different from ours. We blame him for not measuring up to our expectations because we don't understand what he is doing. In the midst of catastrophe, we cry out, "Why doesn't God *do* something?"

We remind ourselves that God has indeed "done something"—he has sent Jesus among us.

We then are tempted to wail, "Why doesn't God do something *else?*"

We want Superman, faster than a speeding bullet, to fly in and rescue us immediately. No matter how we crave that idol-image of God, worship it, and demand that it zoom in and do our bidding, that image is false. God will not do our bidding.

In one cosmic event, God drew all the sin from each of us into Christ, and he—the innocent one—became sin for us. This event began in Bethlehem.

I look into the face of our newborn granddaughter, Kaci, sleeping quietly, her infant face the picture of purity and innocence. I cannot even imagine the force of a love that willingly and deliberately took on the darkness and brutality of the evil that destroys all good, and that this powerful act of love began with the birth of a baby.

Would we exchange that gift of God for something else? We freely and blithely exchange gifts for what fits better or pleases us more. Would we exchange Jesus for—Superman?

When I face my students, which gift would I prefer, a mythic superpower or the incarnational reality?

Sometimes I want the rescuer—
    when God works too slowly.
Sometimes I want the revenger—
    when God asks me to love.
Sometimes I want the righteous judge—
    when God asks me to understand.
But when I look at Jesus,
    from Bethlehem to Calvary,
    from the resurrection to the present day,
I know that God has reached out his hand in
        the darkness
    and holds my hand forever in his own.
When you think God isn't doing what he should
        to help you, reach out for his hand. He is
        there.

Because you are my help,
    I sing in the shadow of your wings.

> My soul clings to you;
>> your right hand upholds me.
>>> Psalm 63:7–8

Father,

You dwell in that realm of life
we cannot see,
and what we know of you
is what we read about you,
what others who have known you
tell us about you.
But we also see you in the face of Jesus,
who came, he said, "to show us the Father."
The children walk with us in dark places,
and they fear, as we do, the shadows.
Open the eyes of their understanding
to see the warmth and power of your hand,
reaching out, to grasp and hold them fast.
Help us make real to them
what you have already done
to transform each one of us
and our world.

7 Start Over

Sing to the LORD a new song.
Isaiah 42:10

Forget the former things;
    do not dwell on the past.
See, I am doing a new thing!
    Now it springs up; do you not perceive it?
Isaiah 43:18–19

Therefore, if anyone is in Christ, he is a new
creation; the old has gone; the new has come!
2 Corinthians 5:17

God bless thy year,
thy coming in, thy going out,
thy rest, thy traveling about,
the rough, the smooth,
the bright, the drear.
God bless thy year.
Author unknown

J anuary, the middle month of the school year and the first month of the calendar year, signals with the two faces of Janus a looking back and a looking forward.

When I said to my friend George, "I wish life had a delete key like a computer keyboard," he replied, "The Christian has one." For the believer, forgiveness removes old sins and brings new beginnings.

When I began teaching, I wish someone had told me to follow these rules the beginning of each day, each week, each month, each year, and each stage of my life (God had, but I wasn't listening):

Make the most of what you have; don't lament what you don't have.

Believe in God and believe in yourself.

Don't rush through your life; take time to savor the small things.

Enjoy people; receive them as they are.

Be yourself. That makes it possible for other people to be themselves with you.

Don't sweat the small stuff.

Remember how quickly children grow up; make the most of every day of their childhood.

Don't be afraid; God will give his angels charge over you, to keep you in all your ways.

Above all—trust God. He is faithful.

> Great is thy faithfulness,
> O God my Father.

There is no shadow of turning with thee.
Thou changest not, thy compassions they fail
     not.
As thou hast been, thou forever wilt be.

                Thomas O. Chisholm
                "Great Is Thy Faithfulness"

Faithful Father,
You make all things new,
every year, every day, every moment.
Thank you for the freshness
of new beginnings.
Thank you for the depth
of your forgiveness
that makes it possible to begin again.
For those whose lives have slowed
into tedium,
for those who rush about
in restless unease,
for those weighed down with failure,
for those flying toward catastrophe,
we ask your mercy,
the exercise of your power,
to do what only you can do—
to create within us a deep craving
to start over.

8
Don't Always Expect to Be Thanked

Does the servant get special thanks for doing what's expected of him? It's the same with you. When you've done everything expected of you, be matter-of-fact and say, "The work is done. What we were told to do, we did."

Luke 17:9–10 *The Message*

A college student with an obsession about grades was asked, "What are you going to do when you get out in the real world where they don't give A's anymore?"

It's great to get all A's, to be congratulated, even to be selected as teacher of the year. Occasionally we get a note that reads, "Thank you for the seeds

35

that you planted in my life." Just one note like that makes any teacher feel rewarded. For many reasons, however, we often don't feel rewarded, and we soon get beyond expecting thanks every time we do a good job as teachers.

Have I fully internalized my role, with its expectations and built-in satisfactions, or do I secretly believe that I deserve better than this? Do I envy others who seem to have an easier time—better students, newer equipment, more access to the supervisor, more perks and opportunities? Am I disgruntled in my work? Am I thinking that somebody ought to do something about my situation?

Someone commented to Mother Teresa, as she tended lepers and took care of the outcasts in their last hours of life, "I wouldn't do what you do for a million dollars!" She smiled. "I wouldn't, either," she answered. She is a servant.

On the cross, Jesus said at last, "It is finished." The suffering servant had completed his assignment. Resurrection power and complete vindication followed.

Ask yourself:

What am I here for?
Why am I working?
What are my goals?
How will I know when my work is finished?
Do I want to be known as a great teacher? or count off the years until I can retire?

Jesus answers:

Whoever wants to become great among you
must be your servant, . . . just as the Son of Man
did not come to be served, but to serve.

Matthew 20:26–28

I would like to give every teacher a sign for his
or her desk that says, "How may I serve you?"

Father,

*You know how much I like
to be appreciated.
You have heard my loud lament
when I think nobody notices what I do.
I complain that it is unfair
for one who does sloppy work
to be rewarded equally
with one who has integrity.
I know that you see everything.
You know what my goals are.
Give me a servant heart
and a goal that will be reached
if you say to me,*
"Well done, good and faithful servant."

9

Help Me Understand

For God is greater than our worried hearts and
knows more about us than we do ourselves.
1 John 3:20 *The Message*

Lawanda talked loudly and constantly. She sat in
her place beside the teacher's desk, separated
somewhat from the rest of the third-grade
students. Eight years old and a newcomer to the
school, she would not settle down and participate
normally.

I inquired about her. She and her brother and
mother recently moved to our area from another
state after her father was murdered and her grandmother died. They now live with relatives on a
temporary basis until her mother can get them
established on their own.

What can schoolteachers do for this trauma-
tized child?

They can accept her. She is one of twenty in her class, which is in a unit of six classes. All of the six teachers know her, and they are consistent in their treatment of her. She is expected to keep the same rules the other students keep; when she is unruly, she must face the same consequences that others would face. The teachers are quietly firm and patient. They do not allow her to disrupt the learning of the other students. They have referred her for special help with her problems; they fill out the necessary papers and wait until help can be provided. For now, the classroom teacher has a major responsibility in helping Lawanda adjust. The teacher must

> provide acceptance so that Lawanda can feel normal;
>
> provide instruction day by day in a stable environment;
>
> guide interaction between Lawanda and her also-needy peers;
>
> all this, and teach the third-grade curriculum effectively!

Their consistent program worked. Lawanda moved from an isolated desk to sit beside the other students. She can sit quietly for longer periods of time, working successfully. There have been no miracles; problems remain to be handled by special services, but in less than four months this student has changed her own behavior.

We receive many negative reports about our public school system, but in many classrooms, in many schools, there are Lawandas who find what they need.

> Now to him who can keep you on your feet, standing tall in his bright presence, fresh and celebrating—to our one God, our only Savior, through Jesus Christ, our Master, be glory, majesty, strength, and rule before all time, and now, and to the end of all time.
>
> Jude 24–25 *The Message*

Father-Counselor,

How can we keep quietly stable
in our faith?
Day by day we face a room
filled with individuals
who must learn from books and from life,
whether or not they feel like learning
or I feel like teaching.
I can't let a disruptive student rob the others
of their own opportunities,
and I can't brush aside
the need behind the disruptive behavior.
Give me wisdom to know what to do
and the physical and emotional strength
to do it.

10 comfort Me

Comfort, comfort my people, says your God.

Isaiah 40:1

I will not leave you desolate; I will come to you.

John 14:18 RSV

Even though I walk
   through the valley of the shadow of death,
I will fear no evil,
   for you are with me;
your rod and your staff,
   they comfort me.

Psalm 23:4

Mark went home one day and found his mother dead. She had committed suicide at age thirty-eight.

Lee's brother was killed in a car accident.

Susan's father was murdered.

Two students were killed when their car was hit by a train at an unguarded crossing.

Grief comes into my classroom. Raw, devastating grief stuns the mind. How can I comfort my students when they are hit harder than I have ever been hit? What can I say? How can I go on teaching as though nothing has happened?

Jesus did not say, "I will not leave you desolate; I will explain things to you." He promised "another Counselor to *be with you* forever," not to explain, but to come alongside, to comfort.

What is comfort?

> A loving presence.
> Someone to wipe the tears away.
> Someone to share the loss and understand the tears.

I can give that comfort to grieving students. I must not try to explain the unexplainable, rebuke the grief or minimize its devastation. I must not offer platitudes and false cheer. I must not run away from the presence of grief. I must let the sufferer talk about the one who has been lost.

> Say as little as I have to.
> Listen as much as I need to.
> Make myself available to love, to listen, to show my student that I know he or she hurts.

If tragedy touches one of your students, before he or she returns to school, explain the situation to the class and encourage the students to treat their friend normally, accepting the awkwardness of a changed demeanor. Encourage them to deal with the subject compassionately and honestly should the student need to talk.

Blessed be the God and Father of our Lord Jesus Christ, the Father of mercies and God of all comfort, who comforts us in all our affliction, so that we may be able to comfort those who are in any affliction, with the comfort with which we ourselves are comforted by God.

2 Corinthians 1:3–4 RSV

Father-Comforter,

Every time I have needed comfort,
you have been there.
You did not ignore my anguished questions.
You did not rebuke my angry complaints
of injustice
when the innocent died young and
tired old people lingered in their suffering.
You came to me and brought peace.
You sent your helpful servants
to take over tasks I could not face,
to hold me when I needed strong arms,

to encourage my tears
and to wipe them away,
to ease the harshness of death with flowers,
good food, and loving-kindness.
When my students face tragedy,
let me be there for them,
to say as little as I have to,
to listen as much as I need to,
to be available to love them
and to ease the load at least a little.

Plug In!

But thanks be to God, who always leads us in triumphal procession in Christ and through us spreads everywhere the fragrance of the knowledge of him.

2 Corinthians 2:14

I sometimes use small devices that plug in to an electrical outlet and release fragrance into a room or hallway. These conveniences have refills of different scents that give off a delightful aroma. When I checked one device recently I found that the refill had a plastic seal over it that I should have removed. The seal protected the liquid from being used up, but it prevented the refill from fulfilling its purpose.

I have another type of refill that fits a similar device that has been misplaced. I placed the sweet, powdery refill on a shelf and sometimes I pick it up and smell it, but the scent is self-contained

45

without the electric current needed to release it into the room.

I often visit classrooms, and I can tell quickly if there is a "plugged-in" teacher there. A teacher whose life is plugged in to the power source of the Holy Spirit gives off the heady fragrance of the love of God. He or she sheds abroad the fragrance of the knowledge of God in that classroom. The students breathe it in and are drawn to the source through that teacher.

My life, like that tiny refill, has a limited value on the shelf or under a cover, protected from being used up but not completing the purpose for which it was created.

What happens every month or the guaranteed forty-five days when the refill is depleted? I replace it with another. What will happen when a plugged-in teacher retires? Unless that teacher is replaced with another who knows and is connected to God's love, that fragrance will linger only for a short, sweet interval, and then the staleness of this world will descend on that classroom.

Where will these new refills—these loving teachers—come from?

Pray that the Lord of the harvest will call them forth and send them out, so that through them, too, the fragrance of the knowledge of him will be shed abroad in every classroom.

Except a corn of wheat [a plastic refill] fall into the ground and die [gets placed into the power source to be used up], it abideth alone [its scent will be of little use]: but if it die [is used up], it bringeth forth much fruit [a wide-spreading fragrance].

John 12:24–25 KJV

father,

Thank you for the teachers who brought
the sweet fragrance of your love
into my life.
Thank you for the teachers
in the classrooms
who are connected to your power
and whose lives sweeten the lives
of their students every day.
Freshen them up;
renew the surge of power in them,
that their sweet savor may never diminish.
And from their influence
encourage other young men and women
to join them in this work
of banishing the staleness of unbelief
in every place.

12 Show Me My Gift

Each man has his own gift from God; one has
this gift, another has that.

1 Corinthians 7:7

She came to me after lunch at her church to
thank me for speaking at the women's retreat
that morning. "I don't have that kind of gift,"
she said, smiling. Then she gestured toward the
open door into a classroom.

"My gift is with those," she said, and she indicated a plant over in the corner of the room.

I went closer to examine a thriving plant, different from any I had ever seen, with its tall, thorny
stems and thick green leaves interspersed with deep
red blossoms. "What is it?" I asked her.

"A crown of thorns plant," she replied. "They grow tall, then shed all the leaves and blossoms, leaving only thick stems and thorns."

She touched the plant gently.

"I believe it was this type of plant that was used to crown Jesus when he was crucified. It grows in that part of the world, and I think of him and his suffering every time I see it." She added, "I chose the best one for my Sunday school classroom."

I can never forget the vivid reminder of Jesus' sacrifice, shared with me by his specially gifted disciple, faithful in using her gift to honor him in a unique way. One of us studied words and spoke to a group of people. The other one studied plants and pruned them with care in order to bring a message to the classroom. Each one had a gift and gave it.

Howard Gardner suggests in his theory of intelligence that there are at least seven types of intelligence, undergirding different abilities, or gifts. Frank Wood teaches that our minds are like different types of lenses, each with a different focus on the world. Brain research backs up God's Word in its teaching about the wide variety of gifts given to individuals; no one is left out.

In schools we want to grade a few things and overlook others. If a student reads, writes, and handles numbers well, that student is considered bright. If a student doesn't do those things well, he or she is viewed as less than average.

My students need me to help them discover what they can do; they are already painfully aware of what they *can't* do.

Do not neglect your gift.

                              1 Timothy 4:14

Father,

> *Let me not measure my ability*
> *against others*
> *whose gifts may be vastly different*
> *from mine.*
> *Let me not measure my students' gifts*
> *against others*
> *whose gifts may be vastly different*
> *from theirs.*
> *Show me what is strong*
> *that I may strengthen it more*
> *and use the strength to shore up the*
> *weak places.*

13 Give Me a Carrot

Where can I go from your Spirit?
  Where can I flee from your presence?
If I go up to the heavens, you are there;
  if I make my bed in the depths, you are
    there.
If I rise on the wings of the dawn,
  if I settle on the far side of the sea,
even there your hand will guide me,
  your right hand will hold me fast.

Psalm 139:7–10

Margaret Wise Brown has translated this pursuing love into her charming book for children, *The Runaway Bunny*. A little bunny keeps running away from his mother in an imaginative game of hide-and-seek. The lovingly steadfast mother finds her child every time.

51

"Shucks," said the bunny, "I might just as well stay where I am and *be* your little bunny."

And so he did.

"Have a carrot," said the mother bunny.

For the small bunny, the carrot symbolized the security of his mother's love.

God loves us no matter what, just as the mother bunny loved her runaway. God does not "treat us as our sins deserve or repay us according to our iniquities" (Ps. 103:10). He does not shield us from the consequences of our sins, but he does walk with us through the dark places of our defeats and always welcomes us back home.

Peter denied Jesus, even as Jesus had said he would. One look from Jesus as he was being led away to be crucified brought Peter to tears of repentance. Later, after his resurrection, Jesus sent word to his disciples "and Peter," setting up a meeting place where he gave to his restored disciple a lifetime mission.

How many times should a student disappoint me and I forgive her? Jesus said, "Seventy times seven"—a number indicating no limit, "even as I have forgiven you."

Is God soft on disobedience, then? Should I be tough?

God is tough. He allows the consequences to fall on us. But he is also incarnational. He walks the valley of consequence with us and always welcomes us when we decide to return to him.

I have often thought, as a teacher and as a parent, that my students or my children would be perfect if I could be the perfect person. It brings an odd comfort to realize that God, the perfect father, still has grave problems with his children.

> As a father has compassion on his children,
>> so the LORD has compassion on those who
>>> fear him;
> for he knows how we are formed,
>> he remembers that we are dust.
>>>> Psalm 103:13–14

Father,

When my students don't try,
I am disappointed;
I know what they will face if they fail.
Help me to "welcome my students back"
as many times as they need it,
because you have never given up on me.
You always welcomed me home
and gave me a carrot
of joyful acceptance and loving security.

14
Please Don't Say "It can't Be Done"

The well is deep . . . You don't have a bucket
. . . You can't draw water . . .

John 4:11 author's paraphrase

I can do all things through Christ who strengthens me.

Philippians 4:13 NKJV

saw her yesterday. The slender high school student, sixteen years old, kept her head down on her desk, apparently sleeping. At the end of the class period, after all the students had left the room, I asked her teacher about the young woman.

"She just found out that she's pregnant by her own father. She has been removed from her home by a protective social service agency, but she calls home several times a day, begging to go back. When she came in today, I asked if she felt like working. She answered, 'No,' and I told her to put her head down and rest. She has enough on her mind right now."

This realistic, compassionate veteran teacher believes in his students. He gives them time and space to begin to trust him, then guides them firmly and knowledgeably into practical learning goals: to read, to fill out job applications, to begin to work confidently in the classroom and at a paying job for part of the school day, to experience the mainstream of life and become confident that they can make it.

In the same room was an autistic teenager to whom the Department of Mental Health had assigned a "shadow" to stay with him all day in order to protect him and other people from his violent outbursts. The visible and reassuring presence of that strong man, the shadow, reminded me of the Holy Spirit, whom God has sent alongside us, to protect, teach, help, comfort, reassure, and guide.

Oswald Chambers says that "the thing that taxes almightiness is the very thing which we as disciples of Jesus ought to believe that He will do."

Can I believe that a young woman can be rescued from an incestuous household?

Can I believe that an autistic young man, prone to violence, can be taught in a high school classroom?

Can I believe that I, a teacher, can face the challenges I have to face every day without breaking apart?

Can I believe that God cares and that he can make a difference? I pray that my response will be the same as the father who brought his son to Jesus to be healed:

I do believe; help me overcome my unbelief!
                                    Mark 9:24

Father,
        Forgive me that I am slow to believe
                that you can do
        anything for those young people.
        I want to rip apart systems
        that create incestuous and violent homes,
        that allow violence to touch the innocent
        in our schools and our neighborhoods.
        The well is deep, Lord.
        How can even you draw anything from it?
        You have nothing to draw with!

No, I impoverish my understanding
of your work
because I forget that you are almighty.
I am so conscious that I am not almighty
that I forget that you are!
The impoverishment is in me, not in you.
Keep me from sinking back into helplessness
and saying that it can't be done.
Let me look away from that deep well
and look at Jesus,
who alone can draw the water of life.

15 Breathe Deeply!

You let the world, which doesn't know the first
thing about living, tell you how to live. You
filled your lungs with polluted unbelief, and
then exhaled disobedience. We all did it . . .
It's a wonder God didn't lose his temper and
do away with the whole lot of us. . . . Instead,
. . . he embraced us. He took our sin-dead lives
and made us alive in Christ.

Ephesians 2:1–5 *The Message*

reathe in unbelief—breathe out disobedience.
Breathe in faith (belief)—breathe out obedience. How often do we expect our children
(and our students) to do what we say, and how
often do we observe, to our chagrin, that they are
imitating what we do?

Paul, in Philippians, doesn't tell us that we can be happy, or how to be happy. He simply and unmistakably shows us that he *is* happy! Even in prison, with his future uncertain, in uncomfortable, limited circumstances, with many cares and concerns pressing on him about his friends in the churches, in *all* circumstances he had learned, not only to be content, but also to be filled with joy.

What am I teaching with my attitude? "You can be happy—joyful"? or "Life is tough. You have to grit your teeth and bear it"?

Our little granddaughter Anna did not talk until she was almost three years old. We were concerned and even consulted a speech therapist. Anna understood everything we said to her, but she spoke only a few words, using in place of words her own very expressive gestures to get what she wanted. We encouraged her in every way we could to get the words out, but she would not speak.

Now, at five, she is highly verbal. She loves to talk on the telephone, and you can see her mother in every gesture! During those non-talking years she watched and listened to her parents and her brother talking on the telephone and to each other. When she was ready, she talked as they did.

Children of deaf-mute parents must learn to overcome their silent role models. Their speech patterns must be developed from other sources.

What are my students learning from watching me? To smile and speak kindly, or to frown and complain? Will they freely copy me, or must they overcome my example and seek more positive role models?

We are very conscious in our society about pollution-free environments. We pass strict regulations about clean air. Several years ago our high school had to spend a lot of money to get rid of asbestos in an older part of the building. The tests taken of the breathing climate in the classrooms indicated that asbestos levels were too high for safety.

What are my students breathing in from me? Can I cheerfully say to them, "Take a deep breath!"?

May the God of hope fill you with all joy and peace as you trust in him, so that you may overflow with hope by the power of the Holy Spirit.
Romans 15:13

Father,

I need "breathing lessons."
Remind me to breathe deeply,
drawing in your love,
your joy,
your peace,
so that the flow of your Spirit
will also touch my students.

16
Teach Me Self-control

But the fruit of the Spirit is . . . self-control.
Galatians 5:22

Terry, eleven years old, started a fight with another student. I separated them, but Terry, in an outburst of temper, ran out the door of the portable classroom and headed into the adjacent woods. The other students and I went in search of him; he returned, still angry. We sat together on the steps outside.

I had called his mother to let her know what was happening. She told me, "I can't do anything with him. His father is the only one who can handle him, and he's out of town. Just do what you have to do."

"Terry," I said to the boy, "I can take over and force you to behave, or you can take over and make up your own mind to conquer your temper. If I do it, you will just depend on me or someone else to take over. You decide. I'll leave you here to think about it. Promise me you won't run away again."

He promised.

Lunchtime came.

"Are you in control enough to go with us to the lunchroom, or would you rather I bring your lunch here?" I asked.

"I'd rather eat alone."

It took two hours for Terry to work through his conflict, but he did it. When he returned, he said, "I still don't like him, but I won't cause any more trouble."

And he never did. He managed his own behavior in that class.

It is difficult to hear that only I can solve the problem I have with myself. Jesus said a lot of hard words. I have wondered why Jesus did not ease up on his hard words to the rich young ruler, who "went away sad, because he had great wealth." Jesus had commanded him to sell everything he had and give it all to the poor, and he simply could not face that total abandonment to Jesus (Mark 10:17–22).

Jesus didn't call him back. He let him leave. Did he later come, after he thought it over? Was he one of the thousands at Pentecost who repented, then brought all they had to share in common with the other believers? Was he one of those scattered abroad by persecution? Did he rethink his priorities and return to the Master?

The Bible doesn't tell us the end of the story. But Jesus always made clear that all of us must decide for ourselves who will control our minds and our actions.

The Bible reiterates hard words about self-control:

> Better . . . a man who controls his temper than
> one who takes a city.
>
> Proverbs 16:32

Father,
  I must abandon my right to my own way.
    I must yield up control
      of my natural and selfish desires.
    I ask that you change the root within me
  so that I may serve you with glad abandon
    and demonstrate the fruit of your Spirit
      that is self-control.

17
Salvage Me!

In quietness and trust is your strength.
Isaiah 30:15

A young minister suffered a complete breakdown early in his career. In order to get his life together, he went to a quiet fishing village and began to teach school. In those seven years, he says, "I became a Christian in the real sense of that word."

As he adjusted his pace to the children and to the hardworking fishermen, his heart began to rest in God. Now when you see him, you notice that his eyes are kind and that they see clearly. His manner is gentle. He hurts with people whose pain he recognizes. His life is practical as he deals with ways in which to encourage and help other people. His speech is direct and without pretense.

After I had worked twenty years in churches, my own life fell apart. In the aftermath, my husband and I left a full-time pastorate. I began to teach students in a small-town high school. Like me, that first group of students had known overwhelming failure. Some of them were hesitant and sullen. Others were tentatively hopeful. Some were passive and withdrawn.

With them, I met God in the marketplace. As Oswald Chambers says in *My Utmost for His Highest*, God "had to destroy my determined confidence in my own convictions and reveal the depths of my ignorance." I had no glib certainties about education or about life. I saw my students not in terms of labels but as individuals. I worked with them to find out what they could do in ways that would make it possible for them to learn successfully.

I gave myself to God and he used me for good, even in my brokenness. I discovered that God will not despise a broken and contrite heart (Ps. 51:17).

Our father,
> You know how to salvage wreckage.
> You have brought us through failure
> and success
> and in both you have protected
> what could be saved.
> We thank you for this.
> Help us to see the treasure buried
> in the garbage dump.

18 Be like Me

Despise not the day of small things.

Zechariah 4:10

Unless you change and become like little children, you will never enter the kingdom of heaven.

Matthew 18:3

mall Rachel lined up with her first-grade class, ready to go to the computer lab for individual assignments. When I stepped into the classroom to visit the student teacher, Rachel saw me and moved over to put her arm around my waist.

I needed that little girl that day. I missed my granddaughter Anna, who had recently moved two thousand miles away. Rachel and I walked together down the hall, my arm around her shoulder and her arm encircling my waist. When I told her that

I missed my granddaughter, she grinned cheerfully and said, "I'll be your granddaughter today." When we returned to class, she pointed toward a little boy across the room. "That's my boyfriend. Can you be his grandmother too?" I left the school that day cheered up by a very special little girl.

I saw in her the natural affection and the spontaneous acceptance that is part of the childlikeness God wants to see in me.

Thank you, Rachel, for showing me the love of a child. You reached for me first, and then we walked together.

Lord,
I have lost the simplicity Rachel possesses.
I put up barriers that block
the childlike faith and spontaneous love
you want me to have.
Thank you for the children.
Open my eyes to see in them
what you want me to become.

19
Say Good-bye

Jesus wept.

John 11:35

Jimmy died last Friday at the age of thirty-seven. He was fifteen when I taught him in the ninth grade.

I saw the notice of his death and called his mother. Jimmy fell asleep driving his car home from work, ran off the road, and went into a ditch, where the car caught on fire. He was his mother's youngest child. His own three children, his mother said, "look just like him," with their black curly hair and small features.

Jimmy had a speech-hearing defect that gave him social and learning difficulties as he grew up. When he came into my high school class, he was struggling to overcome some of those problems. His mother proudly told me that he had become a meat cutter—"the best!" He was a loving family man and an active member of his church.

Ten years after I taught Jimmy, he went to a great deal of trouble to find me, in another city, and to visit me to say thank you for being his teacher.

Good-bye, Jimmy. You taught me more than I could ever have taught you.

Praise be to God that death is not the end!

And regarding the question, friends, that has come up about what happens to those already dead and buried . . . First off, you must not carry on over them like people who have nothing to look forward to, as if the grave were the last word. Since Jesus died and broke loose from the grave, God will most certainly bring back to life those who died in Jesus. . . . And then there will be one huge family reunion with the Master.

1 Thessalonians 4:13–17 *The Message*

Father,

It is hard for me to let Jimmy go.
I think of his young wife
and three young children.
I think of his parents,
his brothers,
his sister.
Each of us who cared about Jimmy
has to turn him loose,

set him free,
let him go.
Thank you that in each separation
we know that we do not walk alone
and what we share together
is never really lost.

20 forget the clock

But the priest and the Levite passed by on the other side, leaving the wounded man unattended.

Luke 10:31–32 author's paraphrase

A seminary professor told his class members to meet him at a certain point on campus. What they were not told was that different groups in the class had different schedules to follow.

Group one had fifteen minutes to get to the meeting place across campus, group two had forty-five minutes to get there, and group three was told to get there any time that was convenient.

The professor then persuaded other students to station themselves at a variety of campus locations and to play roles of needy people seeking help. One faked an injury, asking for assistance in getting first aid. Another pleaded a family emergency with which he needed help. A third asked, "Could I please talk to you?"

None in the first group helped any of the three but instead ignored the pleas and hurried on to their appointment. A few in the second group stopped briefly to lend some assistance. All of the students in the third group stopped to help those who asked for their assistance.

In this way, the professor had his students in the first two groups face their choice of priorities: keeping to their demanding schedule or showing compassion to the people they met.

That trick assignment makes me uncomfortable. I have so many obligations on my calendar that I am tempted to avoid any situation that threatens to interrupt my program. I am also tempted to wonder how Jesus could understand the pressures of our modern society.

Then I remember his three years of public ministry. From the age of twelve he knew that he had to "be about his Father's business," but he lived in Nazareth and followed the pace of village life as though he had all the time in the world to do God's work. We assume that he spent the first thirty years of his life developing normally and as a young adult worked as a carpenter to support his mother and family.

Once he entered the work for which he was called, however, he was thronged by people grabbing at him, calling to him, crowding around him wanting everything: explanations, healing, attention, teaching, and argument. He never appeared to be in a hurry. In personal encounters he talked to individuals about the deepest questions in their hearts, even questions they did not know how to put into words.

Why do I think that everything I have to do is so compelling that it must take precedence over any level of human need? Perhaps because I have a different notion of "my Father's business."

In a children's sermon I heard once, a boy named Dylan helped tell the story of the feeding of the five thousand. "They were so hungry they cried," he said.

Literal hunger pangs torment many in our country and around the world. Even more individuals are desperately hungry for love, acceptance, affirmation, a feeling of value and significance, companionship and belonging.

I shrink back from the sheer enormity of human need. Since I can't do everything, I sometimes choose to do nothing.

It is not the "Father's business" that I try to do everything. It also is not his will that I do nothing. It is his will that I should obey him.

My food, said Jesus, is to do the will of him who sent me and to finish his work.

John 4:34

Teach me to do your will,
for you are my God;
may your good Spirit
lead me on level ground.
Psalm 143:10

Father,

I am not always sure what your will is.
I cannot always tell the difference
between the urgent and the essential.
Show me the way I should go.
Let me hear the cries I should heed
and tune out the clamor that is unessential.
Never let me forget that you are
in command.
I am your servant;
therefore, you are to assign me the task.
I will trust your perfect timing
for your specific task.

21 Recognize My Value

The kingdom of heaven is like treasure hidden in a field, which a man found and covered up; then in his joy he goes and sells all that he has and buys that field.

Matthew 13:44

In a cluttered storage room in a school building, custodians found a box of small statuettes donated for school awards. Tossed aside and long forgotten, the box was old and covered with dust.

An art teacher, searching for materials for student projects, looked through the odds and ends of trash to be discarded and opened the battered box. Examining the contents more closely, she took the box to the school administrator.

To the astonished delight of the school, an appraiser discovered that the small statuettes were made of gold. When they were given to the school, their value was not recognized.

When Lee was born with Down's syndrome, the doctor suggested to his parents that they leave him in the hospital and the doctor "would take care of it." Taking him home, the doctor felt, would impose too great a burden on the family. The parents ignored the doctor's advice. Lee is now twenty-one years old and a joy to his family. He has been a discovered treasure in their lives.

Years ago an alcoholic mother and her troubled family of four children moved into our neighborhood. The oldest son was seventeen years old. Our son got to know him, saw his interest in music, and invited him to join the youth choir in our church. We quickly discovered that this young man was indeed "solid gold." He found his way; he and his beautiful wife now share a successful and influential ministry in God's name.

Several years ago the brilliant, well-educated, highly respected president of a well-known college retired from his profession. The tributes given to him included recognition for his foster mother, who rescued him from the trash can where he had been thrown away. A loving woman saw the value of an infant, took him into her own family, and nurtured in him every ability he had. Trash, tossed aside, became treasure, enriching many lives.

Jesus himself was not considered of high value among those who saw only the surface of his life. When Philip met him and urged his friend Nathaniel to come and meet him too, Nathaniel answered in surprise, "Why? Can anything good come out of Nazareth?" (John 1:46 author's paraphrase).

Even the childhood acquaintances of Jesus, when they heard him preach, asked in astonishment, "Where did this man get all this? Isn't he the carpenter, son of Mary, brother to a large family?" And they took offense at him (Mark 6:2–3 author's paraphrase).

Our grandson Andrew had a third-grade pen pal who wrote to him about his hobbies and his best friends and included a picture with a P.S.: "This is what I look like, except I have all my teeth." God sees us "with all our teeth"—whole, perfect—and he will make it possible for us to see others the same way.

Man looks at the outward appearance, but the LORD looks at the heart.

1 Samuel 16:7

Father,

I, too, look on the outward appearance.
I assume an attractive child
from a good home
has more potential

than a child who has many disadvantages
to overcome.
Forgive my foolish ways.
Let me recognize the infinite worth
of every child
and nurture the abilities that sometimes
only you are able to see.

22

Look Up!

I lift up my eyes to the hills.
   From whence does my help come?
My help comes from the LORD,
   who made heaven and earth.
                              Psalm 121:1–2 RSV

When I visited my chiropractor recently, he said to me, "Have you noticed that when you look down a lot, you get depressed? Try lifting up your head and notice how that quickly lifts your spirits!"

He went on to remind me that the Bible frequently reminds us to throw back our heads and raise our arms and hands when we pray. He added, "There is a center in the brain that relates mood to the position of the neck. Tilt your head down, and the brain kicks into depression. Lift it back, and the mood is changed."

I have often noticed that depressed people look down a lot. Their body language is droopy, like a weeping willow tree.

In my daughter's ninth-grade classroom the ceiling is covered with a fluffy-looking, soft "popcorn" type of foam different from the other ceilings in the building. Each semester the students look up at the ceiling, fascinated by the difference.

When he was a few months old, we took our first grandson outside and showed him the stars. We sang "Twinkle, Twinkle, Little Star" and got excited when he pointed up and tried to say "star." Every time we walk outside at night I remember that baby and his first experience with the night sky.

My friend Becky Swanson and her husband, Don, searched for a mountain lot on which to build their house. Near Lake Lure Don exclaimed, "That's it! Look at that view!"

Becky said, "What are you talking about? I don't see anything special about this place."

Don and the realtor laughed at her. "Look up, Becky! You aren't seeing what is right in front of you!"

She lifted her head. Above and beyond them spread out a spectacular view of the Smoky Mountains, exactly the spot they had come to find.

Look up—away from the fog and confusion at the lower levels, away from the dirt and grime around our feet, away from the darkness and evil gaping beneath us. Look up into the light, into the face of God, who made the heavens and the earth.

> Who is like the LORD our God,
>> who is seated on high,
> who looks far down
>> upon the heavens and the earth?
> He raises the poor from the dust,
>> and lifts the needy from the ash heap.
>>> Psalm 113:5–7 RSV

father,

> *When I bow my head in despair,*
> *I am tempted to give up.*
> *When I bow my head in repentance,*
> *your hand is upon me*
> *to lift me up.*
> *When I lift my head to praise you,*
> *you spread before me the temple*
> *of your holiness,*
> *the beauty of your creation,*
> *the power of your glory.*
> *O Lord, our Lord,*
> *how majestic is thy name in all the earth!*

23
Share My Freedom

Blessed is the nation whose God is the LORD.
Psalm 33:12

For lack of guidance a nation falls.
Proverbs 11:14

Righteousness exalts a nation,
but sin is a disgrace to any people.
Proverbs 14:34

July 4, Anywhere, USA: The menu is simple and the mood is relaxed. There are loud, boisterous, colorful celebrations with flag waving—and flag burning. There is freedom to speak and freedom to keep silent.

The politicians extol our virtues as we celebrate our right to "do as we please." Is this freedom? What is freedom? Is it freedom *from,* or freedom *to*? It is freedom from tyranny and oppression. It is freedom to build what is new and valid.

The celebration on one July 4th featured flags parading down the aisles of the church as a storm drove the ceremony into the church building from the statehouse grounds nearby. Does not the storm always drive the nation into the church?

Countries formerly suppressing religion now openly embrace help for the moral, spiritual, and economic breakdown of their systems. South Carolina's former governor Carroll Campbell said, "The heart of freedom is in the heart of God," echoing James Madison who wrote, "He who would be a citizen of a moral society must first of all be a subject of the divine power."

We once encouraged our students to sing "God Bless America." God has blessed us beyond the brightest dreams of those who founded our country. Will he continue to bless us without our accountability to him, personally and collectively? No nation that forsook his righteous laws has ever stood.

How are students to learn that the greatest freedom lies in obedience? How shall my students learn of the value of their freedom? Must we lose it before we learn to cherish it?

Give to Caesar what is Caesar's, and to God
what is God's.

Matthew 22:21

Father,
   I have never known what it is like to live
      in an oppressive political system.
   The flag and the freedoms have always
            been mine.
   I cherish both, but I don't think
            about them much.
         Like my students
   I take for granted the sacrifices of those
         who died carrying the flag
         to preserve that freedom.
      We owe our freedom to you,
   for you have preserved our nation
         and caused us to prosper.
   We are threatened with the loss of our freedoms
            because we have lost sight
         of our central core of reverence
      for you, source of light and truth,
the one who makes it possible for us to live our lives
            with integrity and obedience.
            Wake us up.
      Show us the next step we can take
   to return to you and to walk in your ways.

24 Mind the Light

In him was life, and that life was the light of men. The light shines in the darkness, but the darkness has not understood it.

John 1:4–5

I am the light of the world. Whoever follows me will never walk in darkness, but will have the light of life.

John 8:12

If then the light within you is darkness, how great is that darkness!

Matthew 6:23

Harold Gray, who served a term in prison for his conscientious objection to World War II, wrote, "The world goes forward because in the beginning one man or a few were true to the light they saw and by living by it enabled others to see."

Emily Dickinson wrote:

> We grow accustomed to the Dark
> when Light is put away . . .
> The Bravest—grope a little
> and sometimes hit a Tree
> Directly in the Forehead.

Have we grown so accustomed to the dark in our society that we have given up our search for light? Worse yet, have we grown to prefer the darkness rather than the searchlight of God in our lives?

Our church, ten miles outside the city, is far beyond the glow of streetlights. Before we put up strong lights on tall poles, we had to endure total darkness on the nights when no moon shone across the parking lot. Those who locked up the church had to grope blindly to find their parked cars. They soon learned to bring flashlights!

Even when all lights go out in a snowstorm, the pure whiteness of the snow takes on a light of its own and lightens the profound darkness. Forgiveness causes our scarlet sins to become as white as snow. This purity picks up the reflected light of Jesus in our lives.

A sign on a sundial states, "Mind the Light." God's presence in us provides that inner light that guides our path. But we have to recognize its presence and mind the light—pay attention to it and discern the direction in which it points our footsteps.

Quakers learn how to practice "waiting for the light" before speaking in their gathered assemblies. How can we learn to "listen in the silence" and receive the light that is given? How can we come under holy obedience and follow the light, however faint, that we are given?

We wait for the light, then ask for the strength to follow it.

In our schools, when we face the evidence of darkness, we can send up a swift prayer: "Father, show me the light that is shining on this situation. Show me the way through this. Give me the strength to follow what I see."

The path of the righteous is like the first gleam
    of dawn,
  shining ever brighter till the full light of day.
But the way of the wicked is like deep darkness;
  they do not know what makes them stumble.
                            Proverbs 4:18–19

When we trust in him, we're free to say whatever needs to be said, bold to go wherever we need to go.
                            Ephesians 3:12 *The Message*

Father of all light,
    *Forgive us for receiving the darkness
    when we could walk in the light.*

Forgive us for blocking the light
when it would shine through us
to illumine the path of those who stumble.
Fill the lamps of our lives
with the oil of your Spirit,
and with a spark from your altar
set us to glowing in the night.

26
Take Time to Be Quiet

He makes me lie down in green pastures,
he leads me beside quiet waters,
he restores my soul.

Psalm 23:2–3

Come with me by yourselves to a quiet place
and get some rest. So they went away by themselves in a boat to a solitary place.

Mark 6:31–32

Go to your private room and, when you have
shut your door, pray to your Father who is in
that secret place.

Matthew 6:6 JB

When I began teaching, student needs clam-
ored and threatened to swamp my attention full time. Since my own family had
needs too, I decided that I had to complete my
work at school before coming home. I also had to
leave the pressing concerns there so that when I

came home I could be "all there." At times, however, frustrations would go home with me. My
youngest son, Charles, seeing my face, would ask,
"Mama, do you have a headache?"

I had to answer quickly, "No, but I've had a bad
day. Give me an hour and I'll be all right." He
understood.

God understands too. We can come into the
quiet place loaded with frustrations and release
them to God, seeing each concern as a balloon,
wafting upward, popping as it rises. In the quiet
place God will lift every load from our hearts.

To bring that solitude into our lives is one of
the most difficult disciplines of the Christian faith.
Even though we may have a deep desire for solitude, we bring our own chaos with us and find it
hard to get quiet. The clamoring concerns are like
noisy, demanding people crowding around the door
we have closed for our time alone with God. The
distractions knock loudly, but after a while they
learn that the door is closed and they can't get in.

> In repentance and rest is your salvation,
>   in quietness and trust is your strength.
>   Isaiah 30:15

Father-Shepherd,
    Thank you for the green pastures
        and quiet waters
        you have prepared for us.

Thank you for the welcome you hold out
when we come into your presence
to rest a while.
You hear the clamoring voices that beg
for our attention.
You see the reaching hands
that hold us back.
You see the deep places
of our longing for quiet,
our hunger for rest,
our need for replenishment
in the peace of your presence.
Give us strength to turn away
from the clamor
and walk into the quiet
where we can be alone with you
so that we can take that quiet
with us into the remainder of the day.

26
Lift Them Up in Prayer

As for me, far be it from me that I should sin against the LORD by failing to pray for you.

1 Samuel 12:23

Several times this year I have been present in an elementary school when the morning announcements have been made over the intercom. The principal gives the announcements, one student leads in the pledge of allegiance to the flag, and then the principal instructs the students and teachers to spend one minute in silence. Each time I closed my eyes and used the time to pray for each person in that building.

This moment of silence took the place of audible, token prayers acceptable to the greatest number of people. Even those innocuous prayers sparked controversy in the schools, for they acknowledged a higher power and offended parents who did not

believe in God or parents who believed that official prayers had no place in public institutions.

Those who believe that God hears prayer always bring prayer with them into every place as they silently lift up the needs they see to the God who cares. Such intercession is invisible, completely legal, private, powerful, and essential if we truly want God to enter the life of a child, a colleague, a parent.

"Father, meet this need" is a swift and soundless cry to the One who is always listening.

Douglas Steere, in *Devotional Classics*, calls intercession "cooperation with God's active love."

For when we hold up the life of another before God, when we expose it to God's love, when we pray for its release from drowsiness, for the quickening of its inner health, for the power to throw off a destructive habit, for the restoration of its free and vital relationship with its fellows, for its strength to resist temptation, for its courage to continue against sharp opposition—only then do we sense what it means to share in God's work.

Call to me and I will answer you and tell you great and unsearchable things you do not know.
Jeremiah 33:3

father of all power,

*You have told us to pray continually,
not in worthless repetitions
for public approval,*

but in private petitions
for those whose needs
break our hearts.
You are ready to hear us when we pray.
You do not ask of your children
that we pray perfectly
but that we pray sincerely.
As we grieve over the problems we see,
may we call on you
and be ready to obey you
when you show us what we can do.

Marjory Goldfinch Ward, formerly an assistant professor at Columbia College and an adjunct professor of gifted education at the University of South Carolina, has over twenty years' experience in public education. She is the author of *Who Will Be My Teacher?* and *Before the School Bell Rings*.